Me, myself and I:
the cross I must bear

Charlie Clements

BookLeaf
Publishing

India | USA | UK

Presentation by *BookLeaf Publishing*

Web: www.bookleafpub.com

E-mail: info@bookleafpub.com

ISBN: 9789358736847

First edition 2023

ACKNOWLEDGEMENT

I acknowledge my Mum, my sister, my Nannie and my Aunty Claire as they are an emotional support for me. My family mean so much to me and I am so glad that they have supported me through thick and thin, so I can blossom into the poet and author I am today. I also acknowledge my son Luke Alexander, my one and only child, my hope and my joy. Lastly I acknowledge my loving boyfriend Nathan who has helped me through many life events and there is more memories to be made.

PREFACE

An autobiography through my poems where life did not go the way I expected. Twenty five years and I have lived so much life. I honestly didn't think I would live this long, but here I am, living and breathing in the Kingdom of God.

A soulless being

Giving a day of life
there is always death,
sucking away a night.
A black face,
but not as we know it.
Its being is soulless
and its eyes are translucent.
It eats the old and sick.
It sees cemeteries wherever it goes,
It feels slow suffering
and it hears screams it creates.
It has no heart,
no bones,
no home
Just a sack of souls to eat,
It's only treat.
A silent killer whenever he must,
but there's something
inside him that cares.
He kills because he cares
and ends the pain.
Misunderstood by other's
crowded emotions,
It's just his job;
Him going through the motions.

His name is not Death.
He has no name,
but people call him it all the same.

Battle of the sun and night

A million Golden wings burn bright,
 sparkling with each wink of light.
Only to parade itself in the day,
 however never at night.
The white beast
 dances way away out of sight,
Twisting and drifting
avoiding the dark's bite.
It is a creature of beauty,
admired by most;
Even the stars
sometimes tend to boast.

But darkness hates its sight,
Trying to swallow it whole.
It growls and howls,
snapping with all it's might,
And suddenly the dark
punctures the beast,
It's mark as dark as coal.
Blood of gold paints the sky
And the beautiful beast;
the Day Soarer
Has lost the battle
and dark has come.

The stars squish out of hiding
And feel sad
that the beast's sparking heart is numb.

But just as the night of darkness
Thought he had won
One gold wing
poked from the earth,
Stabbing the dark
with one mighty jab.
Wailing with shock,
the night tries to grab
But the sun rocks forth
from its death bed.
As more spikes pierce the beast,
The sky fades to grey.
Night is done
And day is ready to play,
As the beast spreads out
its million wings that burn bright
And once again
are sparkling with each wink of light,
The creature does its beautiful dance
And shines its arms into sight

Precious little snowflake

5

Evergreen Earth
is what the snow coats,
A brand new snowflake floats.
Made with love
From the skies above.
Tiny little arms and feet:
Where a family embrace
comes to meet.
A creation that makes anyone smile
Those adoring eyes
as deep as the Nile
Your little pride and joy
Your little girl or boy.

Hope

I'm shattered,
but can rebuild myself.
I'm tattered,
But can sew up the tear.
I'm broken,
But can heal myself.
I'm chokin;
Tears of my own streaming down.
I'm living a nightmare
Always running back
to those who aren't fair.
Does it even to them matter?
That my brain
right now is a scatter.
I'm sorry for what I've done,
But it takes more than one.
I'm not the one at fault
I'll keep that stashed in my vault.
Stuff all the users,
The liars and abusers.
Karma will come,
The time will come
when I no longer feel numb.

A way out of the maze

I feel my world crumbling around me,
Maybe this is just my destiny?
To be miserable,
To feel depressed.
This is worse than anyone could have guessed.
I don't want to do anything,
I'm going through it again.
But this time I reached out for help
And she is "holding" my hand.
These dilemmas call for tissues,
Way more than a game store
running out of comic book issues.
The artist running out of ideas,
The one thing he/she/they fears.
I'm so damaged,
I've gotten older,
Now there's just layers,
Like an ever-changing maze,
What to do
and where to go is all a haze.
There must be a way out.
I need to get out and about.
Sitting all day
makes it not any better,
So I'll push through the walls

or I'll hose them down to mud.
This guy,
He's one of a kind.
It's because he's staying by my side
And coming along for the ride.
We will get out together,
No matter the weight of the feathers
Of the wings we have grown to get out.
It's going to be okay,
I know this because as of today,
I'm turning my life around,
Soon I'll be in his arms, safe and sound.

Sand to pearl

The little speckled swirl
goes from sand to pearl.
They let go once it grows
wings and leaves,
Parents wondering later
what it achieves.
Your beliefs are part of what shape you
from religious form to coloured hue,
Merely a puzzle piece,
an ingredient of a bubbling brew.
You have the power
 to perceive good or bad.
You are the one
that writes upon your pad.
An author of your own destiny
And although in the grand scale
you are mini,
You are mighty as long
as you say and think it.
Results will not happen overnight,
You need to take life bite by bite.
Patience will be prevail and praise
And with the time
you took of many days,
You will find the thing,
person or place you crave.

Breaking away to be free

Necklaces of silver and gold,
Never to be sold
but broken off and cut up,
The stress was too much,
Hearing their voices,
Badgering me over my life choices.
One key laid on the table,
Where it all started;
Where my true self parted.
I lost myself that day,
In every single way,
But at the time saw
 picking up that key
To be the start of the true me.
I had the ability,
To take back what I thought I lost,
But I chose to delve deeper
into spirituality, sexuality and lust,
Oh how I thought I could trust.
They were all mixed and confused
And I was messed up.
I made links
That didn't even connect.
A self contract to burn,
Where I believed I was whole

without men.
A curse I put on myself for 3 years,
But trying to break it only brought tears.
I wore my independence ring
 I got given
for my 18th birthday,
Only to have it smashed
under my own boot with rage.
I smashed my lover's ring
of stoned amethyst,
I returned my ex-boyfriend's bracelet
that I wore on my wrist.
Break the cycle,
Break the curse,
Make a choice,
So I can rejoice.
The gaping hole I filled
with all sorts of things
I finally found that only God
 can fill that void for me
and I love Him unconditionally.
Now I can learn to heal,
Now I am protected from harm
Because I believe that Jesus
 was born in a barn.

The mindset matters

I plan for the future,
But no matter
what I can do
I can go no further.
The present is all we get,
The feeling of living
 in the past is regret,
As our minds
tend to fret (depression).
Everything happens for a reason,
Even through the change
of season to season.
They won't always happen
the way you want them to,
But never fear;
don't feel blue.
Change and uncertainty
is what makes up this world,
Among other things
like in a cocktail swirled.
I'll show you I'm stable,
As long as I'm willing and able.
To get my son back,
I know via God I'm on the right track.
Even when things don't pan out,

What I've learnt
is that it's ok to shout.
Rage built up
will cause you to be unhealthy;
This could even lead
to you being unwealthy,
Luke undertaking
ridiculous shopping sprees.
Without the lows in my life,
That made me be in a lot of strife,
I would not be who I am today,
And I am happy being me;
the true me to never betray.
The mindset matters,
for if it is fixed,
You'll stay in your habits.

Uphill battle

I am not experienced
in the ways of inspiration,
However my God is,
the one of all creation.
I love to see people smile and succeed,
Success used to mean to me money,
yes, indeed!
Now it means giving it your all,
Having goals no matter how small.
I am tired of the uphill battle
of mental health,
But with awareness,
insight and stealth,
I can beat any challenge
of my mind,
For we are all
one of a kind.

Weak wings wisdom

Frost-tipped bare branches
Are clothed with traditional pink jackets
Stretching their arms out to the sun
To melt the soft dew off
to entice the residents coming back from the
south.
The tweeting of the birds
Signals the chosen tree of the season
And the leader with the sharp beak
Perches on the most dressed mannequin
Generous with its accessories.
On the contrary
The young willy wag tail
with the weak wing
Takes a rest on a tree
only wearing it's frilly undergarments.
The birds laugh at Weak wing
As the selection of her home
is bland to compare.
But the bird just flies in a zig-zag
To gather the trusty timber
to structure her bed.
Lukewarm twigs
she weaves into an upside down crown
And with much fatigue

tucks in her head
And sleeps with great patience and wisdom.
The other birds leave her alone,
Mocking her choice still
 but are shocked when she is right.
They come visit out of curiosity
And find Weak wing perched proudly on her
branch,
clustered with brilliantly proud pink blossoms:
The poshly dressed tree with a beautiful dress,
necklace, clutch and matching hat.
 The birds applaud the willy wag tail
and ask if they can take nest on her newfound
home.
She nods and chirps a sweet approval
And her family have finally been reunited with
her.
Surprises of new mouths to feed
Are filled up with scrumptious worms
And the mothers are full of lullabies
Deep in their small hearts to deliver to their little
ones.
Summer is hot on Spring's delicate wings
But in the moment of right now, Spring has
successfully sprung.
Being a Mama bird now herself,
The Willy wag tail had to be brave.
To give her little one
His best chance

She let him go out into the world
To be raised by other birds
And they will be reunited one day
As mother and son.
But until then,
She fights to take flight herself,
Being nudged that her tree was pretty,
But now she needs to bloom too
And she is encouraged
That she will very soon.
She believes this
And so she keeps on flapping
And one day
That weak wing of hers will be gone.

R.I.P Hoodie

Well that sucked,
I thought he loved me.
I thought he would fight.
The hoodie that he left me,
In confidence I'd take care of it...
It's dead.

The sweatshirt he said is merely just a
sweatshirt.
It's just a hoodie.
It has no zipper.
It's just a hoodie he said
So why when I snuggled it did it make me feel
less dread?

The very idea that it belonged to him
Was enough to give it power,
Enough to give me comfort,
Enough comfort to get me to sleep soundly.

It is just a hoodie now,
Just an article of clothing.
One that is useless to him,
One he disowned.

Uncertain of when he was going to break it off,
Like he broke that zipper,
Trying to get me into it
And failing because it didn't fit.

You can't force something that isn't right.
You can't pretend that everything is fine.
The death of the hoodie was not my end.
It will not break me, but it will make me
stronger.

I wanted to hold onto him just a little longer.
Little did I know,
My grip on him,
My demands of growing stronger as a person...
My evolution as the new me,
That was the thing that broke us.

It was effortless at the beginning,
It was running on a constant high,
But we had to come down eventually.
I didn't read the warning signs.

Reflection is crucial,
Time away is essential.
His love was conditional,
But conditions I could not adhere to.

But if the expectations are to be there 24/7,
Well, how did I really think it could last?
When the reality is more so 6/2?

Very different people indeed,
A very powerful transformation.
Two individuals who took a chance,
Only to see who would take the last dance.

Untamed beauty

This beauty I see;
It is unlike anything I've ever imagined.
I want it
And climb the biggest tree.
Each branch I step onto
The dazzling Necklace of the Sky fades
Just a little more.

When I reach the top
It is no longer.
I am up high
And can taste the last drops of rain
Feel the sun on my face,
I touch the tough bark I cling to
And I decide to go back down.

Although I cannot taste
Or touch or feel
I smile and it does back
As I accept the beauty
The essence of natures many miracles.
Without its rarity
It is no longer special
And if we can touch it we will take it.
We may have conquered the sky

With our metal jets and planes
But we will never claim the wonderous creation
For which we have called the rainbow.

Embracing destiny

The transformation
that I have been going through:
it is exquisite.
Who knew I could feel so safe?
Just by embracing my path
to tread lightly on.
The path of a writer
 is treacherous and long.
It is skinny and bendy,
 with lots of last minute turns,
But what am I waiting for?
I haven't had a better opportunity.
I start today
and watch my creativity flow.
Today is the day
 that I don't put it off.
My greatest piece
that will be for show.
I'll write it, I will.
Just not yet...

I'm excited to start off small
And work my way up.
I'm enthralled to be an author,
But how far can I go?

I'm spreading my wings,
I'm loving the leap,
The day has come
Where my inspiration runs deep.

I see the world,
I see the hope.
I was broken down by my own mind,
Only to find the light.
Now, here I go.
I take flight!

Reflect lovingly

Maybe it's time for you to go away,
I never met a mirror that could be so mean.
Extra kilograms,
Less curve on the waist,
Oh how I wish I could just copy and paste.

Maybe it's time to walk away,
Second look,
This time looking better,
Why mirror, did you make my dimples look
cheaper?
I'll pick a feature and make myself a self love
teacher.

My cheeks,
Third and final,
They are rosy and meek.
Mirror,
Even though you are just glass held upon a
wooden frame,
Somehow you take control of my name
And therefore you are to blame.

No, I won't let you win!
You say I'm bigger than I actually am,

But that's okay
because what I see
 is a mother that carried a bubba.

Yep, that's right, I'm grinnin'!
You say I'm more plump than peplum,
But that's alright,
Because I've got the outfits
that hug myself just right.

As shallow as this may seem,
Self esteem is everything.
The way I feel about myself
Is how I walk, talk and am
 inside and out, regardless if I'm on cam.

So with all due respect,
I'm walking away because I feel fantastic.
Love handles are here to stay,
Because I love who I am.

With love for myself
and then poured onto others,
That's how I slay.
Goodbye mirror
and hello gorgeous, sunny day.

Rendering my love

There's a reason
These people
Keep coming back
To my attention.

These people
That seem to be
Glimmers in the speck
Of my life.

One moment
They are here.
The next
They are gone.

Like ghosts,
Floating through the haze.
Oh I wish
I could erase.

But they stay.
They are not going anywhere.
Just because I block,
Does not mean
Their existence stops.

They live on,
Because I'm not in control.
They move on,
Because I'm not their be all/end all.

I'm just a person
And so are they.
They'll make someone happy one day.
Perhaps they even already have,
Just not in the way I understand.

Letting them go
was easy with help,
But remembering the good
and leaving it at that,
Now that's the real obstacle,
Like the eating of the fat.

You're guilty to indulge,
Because you're guilty to feel happy.
You could not believe
someone to love you,
When are you are so snappy.

But they did and he does
 and you can love yourself too.
It's safe.
It's okay.

It's alright to tuck your own self
in at night.
It's okay to not be perfect every day.
It's safe because you're surrounded by those that
protect and love you.
You walk and talk you and let the rest shine
through.

Growing up so fast

Flashbacks of when I was young
Once I was so small,
And the world was big before me,
Oh how I grew up so fast.

Growing up
I thought I had it so bad,
Poverty and death and disease,
My life was very scary.

I grew up quickly
To know that I was living a dream,
The injustice in the world
Made me want to cry and scream.

But then I was getting older,
Not getting younger,
I thought the world was black
And then fireworks.
But I wasn't getting any younger.

I grew up a little more,
I thought I knew it all,
And I was ripped into.
It wasn't a pretty picture.

Drugs, sex and unsteady figures,
I was lost and then emptied out.
I thought I was a walking zombie.
The medication hit me hard,
Didn't know if I was coming or going.

What I thought was mature,
Actually couldn't be
For someone as young as me,
So I had to stay 23,
Off to the clubs in dresses so skanky.

Losing my self esteem,
Wanting to be grey
in a world of black and white,
It wasn't happening.
But then I found community centres.

I found the love of my life,
After finding connection
But I had to take a chance
On possible rejection.

It is so damn hard,
But I'm getting through it,
Halfway through divorce
And heaps of other s**t.

I'm learning I can't do it alone,
I'm learning I don't know it all,
I'm learning we all got problems,
I'm learning together we can solve them.

The biggest struggle

I'm on the bus,
I leave home
in the early morning,
Wondering why
My stomach is churning.
Living a life
That I could
never have imagined,
Giving up the fight
Because it's not worth
it to lose it all.

The battle in my head
Says forget you
But it also says
I wish you the best.
It's reminding me
of the good times too
But the struggle
is over what I fret.

But then I have learnt to
Not beat myself up
I tried my best.
I thought you were the one,

Now I see you as his father
Nothing more, nothing less.

And I thank you
For the struggles that we fought through,
Even though the biggest struggle
In the end was loving you.

Diamond figurine

35

I feel like I'm crumbly and hard-hearted,
A lump of coal:
That's me.
But the Lord takes His tools
Into His hands
And chips away
At me.

With a chisel,
Chip, chip, chip!
With His hands
He molds me
Like pottery clay.
With His love
He shapes me into a person
I am proud to be.

With all of the pressure,
Stress
And guidance,
He has transformed me
Into a diamond.
But He is not done,
Because now I am a mere stone,
But I am ready

For the next phase.

He is willing to love me
Not because I am well educated
Or wealthy.
He loves me
Because I am His child.
I am His daughter
And I am more of Him
And less of me.

Diamond form,
This is me now,
But I need to stretched,
Taught patience,
Humbled
And all the while,
Give Him the glory.

He loves me
And that's why He
Has turned me into
A diamond figurine.

How the rose got its glow

There once was a rose
That smelled of pure beauty.
But it did not have a colour
That made it stand out.

This rose would shake its leaves
Free of the wintery grip.
It would stand proudly
On its stem,
Its thorns never trimmed
For the Gardener saw her as a gem.

What the rose felt it lacked,
The Gardener did not
And He would reassure her
All the more,
She is a rose
Among thorns.

The rose could not comprehend.
She looked down
And saw her thorns,
But still it did not
Yet click.

A Firefly was nearby
And he was happily buzzing,
Until He saw the rose.
He asked, 'Why no glow?'.

She replied, 'I have no glow
to show, although
My Gardener says I have thorns
and a stem that has me
firmly planted,
From when I was a seedling and
From every moment then'.

'I wonder what it would be like
to be grounded like you',
said the Firefly.
'I wonder what it would be like
to be able to be carried
 throughout the night
And take flight', said the rose.

That is when the Firefly
and the rose buzzed
with a single shared thought.
The Firefly said,
'would you like to fly?'
And the rose nodded.

The Firefly dug under the soil

And tickled her roots,
Until she was free.
He took her on his back,
To the Firefly lit track.
What a ride!

Firefly did become tired,
But this trip had opened
the rose's eyes.
The Firefly asked if he
could take shelter under her petals
As it started to spatter
And the rose agreed.

The Gardener called out
to the rose
And as the Firefly slept,
He emitted a glow.
The gardener could see
this glow
And recognised her at once.

The Gardener was pleased
The rose had made a friend.
She was happy
And as the Firefly awoke
From the chatter,
The rose stayed glowing
Without the aid of the Firefly.

She was full of joy.
The Gardener assured her
And this time
The rose just beamed,
For she was no longer lost,
But she was happy.

Run to you first

You give me strength
That I can't deny
Something about you
Makes my heart want to fly.

I can't help it.
I didn't even earn it.
Your love,
For my struggle it's worth it.

First
I will run to you.
First I will
Believe in the truth.
You are my undying desire.
Yes you are my light
 in my Holy fire.

Give me nothing
And I'll give you everything.
You deserve all the praise.
And I will raise your name.

With you I have no shame
Because you make me sane.

I know my past was dark,
But you made my future bright,
As you ignited my Holy Spirit light.

You are my first love.
You are the beauty of the above.
I no longer fear what is to come
Because you call me your child
And I am dear to you.

Priceless is the price you paid,
Worth more than gold
Was the covenant you made.
I love you Lord
With all my soul.

I love you with everything I have
And for all eternity
I'll keep trying
To love you more.

Trading in the old

This is all I want,
Piece by piece
Taking it all away
To make room for the new.
I'm ready to trade in
What I have for myself
And give it all to You.

I may not get it right
The first time
Or the next
Or the next time after that,
But You love me regardless.

Deleting the stuff
That no longer serves You
Because I want less of me
And more of You.
I don't need my dry bones
To strive anymore.
I just need to lean on You
And that's exactly what I plan to do.

www.ingramcontent.com/pod-product-compliance
Lightning Source LLC
La Vergne TN
LVHW051235200726
843510LV00011B/1573